# Your Turn to Speak!

First published in 2023 by Blue Diode Press
30 Lochend Road
Leith
Edinburgh EH6 8BS
www.bluediode.co.uk

ISBN: 978-1-915108-10-4

Typesetting: Rob A. Mackenzie
text in Pilgrim LT Roman

Front and back cover art: Lady Red Ego / April Hill
Cover design and typography: Rob A. Mackenzie

Diode logo design: Sam and Ian Alexander.

Printed and bound by Imprint Digital, Exeter, UK.
https://digital.imprint.co.uk

# Your Turn to Speak!

## Lady Red Ego

Blue Diode Press
Edinburgh

# CONTENTS

*For every soul I have been blessed to love*
*with all the mouths I have loved you from*

# YOUR TURN TO SPEAK! – THE PROPOSAL

The theatre is filled and the play is announced. Zeus takes centre stage. His booming voice dominates. But then, no, here is Hera and she has something to say. Zeus was lying. The crowd gasps. He was exaggerating. He was simply playing a part. Here, she says, I have the truth.

And so, it begins. Patroclus reveals that he bottomed (shock and horror). Achilles breaks into tears and must be carried away. The Erotes arrive, Aphrodite trailing behind. Sappho eyes him (that's right) from the first row. Even Medea makes a show. And alas, here come the chorus, bursting into harmonious babble! They have a great many things to exclaim and no intention to explain!

*Your Turn to Speak!* gathers classical lovers into a room and encourages them to speak one by one. Not all of them do. Some of them return a great many times, revisiting their own narratives, editing and rewriting. In a way, they are speaking for each other. In a way, they are speaking for themselves.

This is a body of work that examines the movement of power as narrative control is transferred, often being undermined and empowered in the same breath. It dissects the DNA of the love poem, and what it means to perform love as a solitary actor. It considers the futility of answering and the selfishness of conversation. It discovers the innate duplicity of voice. It tries to hold truth in its hands but finds that truth is a substance that only exists in the action of being passed.

In a theatrical culture where romance is associated with comedies, the poems in this work wrestle amongst themselves with tragic sincerity. Indeed, the definition of the tragedy is challenged by the poems just as much as the poems are by the weight of their genre. The "masks" obviously refer back to the stage and the actor, but increasingly align themselves with the voice, and the attempts made by both the reader and the speaker to remove them are generally frustrating, bloody, and at times shockingly easy. Of course, you are reading about yourself just as much as I am writing about myself. A mask is a mirror, after all.

*hushed murmuring*

Did they buy it?

Can we come out?

Hush!

CHORUS (ALL TOGETHER):

Who goes there?

CORYPHAEUS:

No one.

CHORUS:

It must have been the wind.
Or the post-structuralists.
You know how it is.

APHRODITE:

Is that a storm coming?
A tempest?

CHARON:

Is someone coming home?

SAPPHO:

Is someone colonising?

CHORUS:

Hush!

CHARON:

A boat,
on the horizon.

ERIS:

Someone is
coming home.

CORYPHAEUS:

Come on Odysseus,
give me all you've got.
Your best shot,
bound to blind a cyclops.

ODYSSEUS:

It is not
what you were taught.
This noble knife,
down the mouth of a
gift-horse.
Look in it. Gargle and spit.
Cleanse your palate.
Sugar can be opened
like the buttons of a coat
but bitterness lingers
in
the
throat.


POLYPHEMUS:

Don't you tire of wordplay?
It'll be the death of me. Tell me,
why is it worse to eat the flesh
of a white-skinned man than that
of a sheep? Who follows and who
is the wolf that leads? He stuffs me
full of lies until I cry his name:

ODYSSEUS! I AM COMING
FOR YOU! I AM COMING HOME!
HOME IS THE NAME OF THE ANIMAL
THAT I SLAUGHTER AND BLEED OUT!


FATHER!

FATHER!

## MEDUSA:

I hear another voice.
It is coming again,
this hesitant shedding,
the swollen waterbirth
of tongue between lip.
There are many words,
but aphasia comes first,
melting interrelation like
soft metal. Every woman
is bilingual; or at least every
woman who has prayed. I have
long left that temple.
Such is life. Such goes the tragedy of
being left behind by other, paler women.
Poseidon and his phallic philtrum
told me this; that I would be punished.

POSIEDON:

The brute was right.
There must be violence where
there is sight.


ACHILLES:

Winter has arrived.
It was snowing inside,
a stripe of white from
his cheek to his bellybutton.
Arms and legs spread, a five-point pyramid.
My December Angel.
And aren't there more points left,
something about the paper and sheets?
Nothing is whiter than violence.
Nothing is colder than finishing
separately.

The theatre is filled and the play is announced. Zeus takes centre stage. His booming voice dominates. But then, no, here is Hera and she has something to say. Zeus was lying. The crowd gasps. He was exaggerating. He was simply playing a part. Here, she says, I have the truth.

She angles her arms to reveal a babe. We think of Christ, but it is not yet his time. He has already died.
The child rises like a stem, a heavenly helix of a staircase. The child unwinds. One day it will reach us all. One we will all have to
                            step below.
                            These stairs are
                            made of stone. You have
                            cold feet, but there is nowhere else to go.

HERA:

Pull in, deep well
of death, that black
life-giving tunnel. How to
drink without falling?
Lord knows it is
never enough for me.
Never a good enough
reason to leave. He
saved my life when
he made his wife.
Then just like that

he took it back.

ACHILLES:

Just like that.
I thought he might come back,
or at least visit. In the night
I heard him at the windowsill,
tapping. Why would you lock me out?
No, darling, I – threw back the covers
and pried open the glass casing.
Did you get cold while you were waiting?


SAPPHO:

Not all wounds heal.
What is fragmented
will learn to co-exist
with

whatever is in between.

The theatre is filled and the play is announced. Its ears perk up at the sound of its name – *Tragedy* – that hard consonant followed by the G, which melts on the tongue like toffee. It has all kinds of internal rhyme, and sure goes out swinging.

Heart beating, it makes its way onstage. Its palms are sweating. It rehearses its lines, remembers its mother holding its shoulder. *You're a champion*, she told it.

*Damn right I am.* It is coming into the light now. The world is too bright to see beyond the end of its nose. It blinks into the darkness

and the darkness blinks back. Eighty thousand candlelit faces, holding vigil for a body that is still thrumming. *You are because you think? I am because I ache.* A critic waits for the inevitable scene of heartbreak only to look down and realise he has bled through his shirt pocket. He looks up just in time to see the monstrosity crawling across the open hillside, a flame of feeling yet to be contained. It heaves its shoulder blade over its bicep, drags its knees up to its stomach. It struggles against its muscles, a tug of war that sends it sprawling. The crowd cringes, but the critic can't look away. He feels pain in a body that he has never noticed belonged to him. Until now. Until he paid and sat down. Until the play began, and his name was announced.

*Achilles.*

## PATROCLUS:

Things are not what they seem.
Maybe I was his cousin, his friend,
if that makes it easier to believe.
If that is closer to your reality.
Is friendship really further away,
a moon that does not move
the water onto the beach?
Did you never have a friend
that you kept in your chest
until it was punctured
and bled?

CYCLOPES CHORUS:

Round eye.
Pupiled apricot pit,
egg white orbit.
My body is airless space          My body is an empty stage
But now it has been drawn open.
Eyelid, the heavy damask
of skin.
The tassel of eyelash, tugging down
as condensation weeps.
A fine audience,
the whole of Greece.
The sun rises on the Achelous River     Only to set in Megaris.
Achilles loves a dead man
and Patroclus loves a star that burns.
Hold each other
the way I hold vision
in my bone cavity.

The theatre is filled and the play is announced. You come with all your friends, eat dinner backstage. You performed well yesterday; you must perform better today.

More vigour, more fever in the monologue. Pretend you are speaking to yourself. Pretend everyone is naked. Pretend you love this man, the terracotta grin of his face. When he is done, take it and perform again. And again. And again.

CORYPHAEUS:

Now you've done it.

CHORUS:

We did nothing wrong!

CORYPHAEUS:

All right.

CHORUS:

Were we to stay quiet,
nestled between the lines?

CORYPHAEUS:

Is there no way to say
what needs to be said
without giving it all away?
Don't reply. Look, I
make no mockery
of his rage. Yes, it is sacred
the pain against which
I sharpen my blade. Tongue,
shielded cheeks. Things
are not what they seem.
Someone goes to war
and finds themselves
naked. Someone goes
to bed wearing armour.
There are knives everywhere.
A man sits to watch a play
only to find that it is a funeral.
He will die on that hill.

PATROCLUS:

A man goes to a funeral
only to sing the song of nuptials.

CHORUS:

Is that wedding bells?

CORYPHAEUS:

No, no,
this is only the proposal.

# Your Turn to Speak! –
# The Iliad

EROS:

You have
good reason
to be skeptical.
As am I, judging
the distance between
arrow and target, which
makes love to lung.
(Don't get this wrong.)
My bowstring is taut, tense,
let loose and – gods, not this –
I missed.

APHRODITE:

Something persists.

ZEUS:

They say there's no such thing
as a good and powerful man.
Lucky that I am not made
of leg and shoulder blade,
that my body sheds its form
like a snake. They say I became a bull,
a swan, and that wildest animal:
woman. I fucked her under the tree of
knowledge and ruined her for marriage.
Fruit fell around her head and rotted.
Hera waited in the kitchen, slaving over
the roast dinner, knowing full well
I'd be home late. That is power –
the way she knows better than to leave.
They say I was the sun, bearing
illegitimate sons, strangers that
rained like clouds around me. It is
lonely at the top, and I am just a man –
like any other. Just like your brother.

HERA:

I still miss him.
Strange, isn't it,
the love that floats
through life without
a home. He is in the living room,
watching television, in another world.
I cannot cross over
airless galaxies. Love, can't you
see how I am unable to breathe?
My skin will flay from the bone
to build bridges between our planets.
When you step forward,
your foot is on my throat.
You should know
that no apology can ever redeem
what happened here. There is no
forgiveness, only that slow gentle
trickling of narrative. If only I could
sew my soul shut, like you do.

JASON:

Listen. Some women
are made for marriage
and some for dying. Of course
we were once happy. She was golden,
a chariot drawing over the
clouds of my body. I curved
into myself with love.
When we were
fucking she
always looked past me. Maybe
God was on the ceiling. Helios and
her native magic. She gave it all up.
Tell me then why she couldn't give me
this one last thing. Darling, did you really
want a man or did you want a reason
to dissect your brother's body?

And all those tests. Fire-breathing
oxen and dragons and armies that
spent the night slaughtering their friends.
Fields lined with teeth. We have sons,
but nothing grows here. Darling,
she loves me. She makes it easy
to be human. Can you really blame me?
Deep down, there must be a part of you
that still wants me to be happy.


MEDEA:

Fuck these kids.

PATROCLUS:

He looks just like truth.
You would think so too
if you looked down the table
and saw a man like that, the regal
arch of his temple, the cornucopia
of his conversation. I could eat this
meal forever. My lover-king, let me
be the napkin that crumples at
the corner of your mouth. You don't
know how I grip myself, thinking of
the smile you gave me across the room
when we laughed at the same joke. I don't
care about your mother. Let us be together.
If I die in your armor, I would die happy
inside your metal body, your masculine
understanding, those silver bones that
hold me close and ready for the spearhead
of your cock bleeding into my belly.


ACHILLES:

Please no please no please no no not him

PYSCHE:

I suppose every marriage has its secrets.
But these things take their toll. He
seems only to love me from the shadows.
Darling, are you a man or are you made of
fear, the cold glass sphere that warns you
against touching? I see your fingerprints.
I am not a doll, my body will hold
that ache you impregnate and make
it tangible. What I would do to just
taste you. I have imagined your smile,
held that golden arch in my spine
and began to climb that slow, strange ascent
into pragma. Heaven is a place where I
meet your eyes in conversation. You must
know I love you, from my cadence,
my small shifts and habits, the way I
cover my mouth when I eat. We cannot
go on like this, suspending tenderness
in                                 distance.


EROS:

She is too bright to look at.
My wings are not made of wax,
but they melt. I have learned well
from Icarus, who didn't understand
hubris, or how to swim. Curiosity
is a cup you can drown in.

She loves that I care. It hardly matters
what face I wear.

HIMEROS:

I saw you with her.
You two only need time,
that shackle that winds
around my ankles. Your arrows
fall close, but mine fly forever
through trees and over mountains.
Maybe one day there will be a valley,
filling as the ice melts. I will be in that
blue lagoon, letting my breath go.
Filling also. I have evolved gills. It is
the only way I know how to
weather rejection, that unspoken
neglect of budding bulbs. Some flowers
don't bother to wilt and instead return
to the deep underground caverns of
themselves. Our future is that flower;
I open my eyes underwater and see fish that float.
A miracle, that some things still grow.
Things like hope.

ANTEROS:

Forgive me
Achilles.

ANTEROS:

I know which valleys
he means. I saw them
from the window, in
the moving carriage
of your honesty. Yes, darling,
the train was drawing in.
Dundee station, so much
like a palace, all that cheap
white paint and stairs that
escalate above mountain summits.
You said you were waiting
and I believed it, because I
was coming.

CHORUS:

And so it was!
And so it is!
People were speaking
(they were speaking!)
and the room was loud!
It echoed through the walls
(yes it did!) And you couldn't
hear yourself think, but it was
your turn to speak!

SAPPHO:

The magic came again.
It visited my fingertips.
Bed-death, la petite.
The female prefix, a default
for other women to lay
beneath. I have lied.
I have waited. You are not a man,
too refined, the soft jut of your chin,
the narrow bone of your hip. I have
told them other names you go by,
titles like violet and mister and
Achilles. Sir, there is no need
to obscure your body. His breast
fills my mouth like a wine cup about to
spill. I hold my liquor the same way
I hold conversation, the anticipation
of set up, punchline, the white milk
bathing the black outline. Subtext.
My heart, you have heard my language.


APHRODITE:

Yes, I was tomboyish –
climbing trees, scraping knees.
Yes, they put me in a dress. I remember
my school teacher bending over
my desk, teaching me alphabets. Now
I must speak –

Sweetheart, will you weave baskets
of nonce taxonomies so that I may
have a word for this hot, wet love?

ACHILLES:

Warmth came slow,
the sun baking the colonnade stone,
the heart muscle pulsing against the rib bone.
Ocean water which is at first
unbearably cold. I came to tolerate
it like alcohol, the stinging dilation of my
blood vessels. Then the pressure;
the crushing of the pericarp,
the fermenting of the fever,
desire waiting in painted jars.
When did I become so addicted
to the shape of your wit? Which moment
was the one that cemented
that black liquid, the bacchanalian beat that
let me cross from my bed into your pallet?
We should not have spent so much time
sleeping alone.

CHORUS:

Yes, it was about you!
Yes, we were kissing!
Yes, we went the same way home!
Yes, we lived close!
(Hallelujah!)

ZEUS:

A man
like any other.
As it is so often
the truth was
in the middle.

After all,
I must want something.

CHORUS:

Does the conversation
ever truly finish? Another
glass of wine, a cup of coffee,
and you are back in your seat.
Where were we? (Here we are.)
What were we saying? (Only this.)
Ah, yes, you remember
it was turning into November,
and the leaves were dying
that long red death.
They were falling like lovers,
who landed atop each other
and were swept into piles
at the side of the street.
So we could keep walking.
Where does it end?
(It bends, it bends.)
Where are you going?
(On the train to Perth.)
After all, Anteros has
answered (and he has
asked) yet another question.

MELPOMENE:

A wedding is all it takes.
And what is left for a
Bastard-God, the muses
born out of wedlock?
A mask and sword, fit
to slot over my marmoreal
indifference. I will carve
Frank Ocean's ivy into
a wreath. Melpomene. To dance
and sing. You have heard
me chanting. There are monks
nearby, buried in the valleys.
They will have to make way
for lakes. The climate is changing
– or Himeros, as we call him.

CORYPHAEUS:

How did you know it was me?
Did my breasts give me away,
the gentle slope of my face?
Was it bio-essentialist, that concentric
gaze of yours, searching for
one honest voice?

You can find truth,
if you really want to.
It is tucked into the
accordion underbelly
of a mushroom.
According to you
I was playing dress up
and you were Prospero,
here to shock me out of
my crown and robe.
According to you I was
Ariel, begging to be sliced
out of bark in a caesarean
smile. According to you,
my mother left me without
an Isle. But she did. But she did.

ACHILLES:

A bright light.
You came into my life.
There was the tunnel;
a mile-long hollow under
Chinese mountains, electric
white punctuating in intervals.
Living was an ellipsis
that never finished. I used to
believe death was kind.

Pay the past no mind. Surely
we have waited long enough.
These brilliant fireworks
hold their weight in the sky
as I do, braced on my forearms
above you.

CORYPHAEUS:

What would Barthes say?

CHORUS:

He would carry me offstage like a brute!

CORYPHAEUS:

Et tu?

CHORUS:

You would burn my staff and book!

CORYPHAEUS:

And you?

CHORUS:

And we, we sing
from our hearts and chests and throats,
we sing from every cell, we peer through
bars of purple prose, we stick our arms out and wave
our dinner bowls, we rise like an army over the hills
and you,
and you,
and you are our general and we are ready!
We will crush you like a fruit!

CHARON:

I met him.
You can rest.
I have been
asked this before.

SAPPHO (FRAGMENTS):

I          be silenced.
     for women, who followed
through the waters
               out of context
he was a woman          spoke back
   answered          the most important thing
silenced          Achilles can't have it all
        he followed
                    they all followed
     through the waters
searching for new land
                         an island

say its name

.

CHARON:

Since you persist –
yes I carried him across.
You want to know
how it was. Well,
he was not very handsome.
Heavier than I expected.
His spine knocked my
sternum like it was a door.
I would not let him in. You
need a thick skin to work in
customer service.

MNEMOSYNE:

You must remember this
Achilles. There is a river
that I preside over. Lethe
in Hades. Do not drink
from it.

I am still a mother.
Have I not fed you well?
Did I not birth your tragedy,
oiled between hymns and love poetry?
Yes. So drink from me still. Even if
your husband-wife has gone without,
you must drink. You must remember this.

ACHILLES:

Oh, God Patroclus
there you are. I see you now.
I have been looking for you
in the rain, in the mountains,
under the bellies of mushrooms.
I dreamt of this; your forehead
pressed against my neck.
I dreamt and wept. How many
mornings did we spend in the
soft dawn of love, growing past
the limits of our bones? I have been
here, on the other side of the pillow.
I have made my peace.
When you were gone it was
a pain greater than death. To drink water
without pouring your cup felt impossible.
Then I drank
and I remembered.

CHORUS:

Something persists.

APHRODITE:

You too?

PATROCLUS:

Yes,
And you?

# YOUR TURN TO SPEAK! – THE ODYSSEY

POLYPHEMUS:

Are you there? Do you hear me?
Father? Did you birth me?
How did my mother bear it?
My body? My bones? My skull,
which I now know, was too giant
to fit through a nymph's pelvis.
Did she want it? You or I, the
white globe of life, mine, the pupil,
the tunnel into a son, not her species,
not yours, not the ocean's –
who did it? Who carried me
from pederasty to heterosexuality,
from sea to Sicily

and left me there?

                    Why?

                         Sometimes I think I understand him,
                                    my little coloniser,
                always taking the long way around to his wife.
                              These waters make promises.

PATROCLUS:

Achilles, I think that I am like him.
Some kind of deformed thing, composed
by no parent worth noting. If I had not loved you
(I must've always loved you) I would be probably
on that orphan island. I would be

ACHILLES:

with me.
Why talk of what has not occurred?
You fret too much.

I love too much.

It is only just enough. Pray,
let us sleep.

PHILOMELA:

*bird sounds*

CRONUS:

It had to be done.


GAIA:

All boys are good sons.
I even love you, my
hundred handed darlings.
More hands for holding.


CRONUS:

More suns for dimming.


GAIA:

More fathers for castrating.
Pray, learn from him and never
fear your own offspring.

ZEUS:

A man like any other.

Except! Who speaks –

                                                    OURANUS:

                                                    It can't be –

                        APHRODITE:

                    They call me gladiator,
                well-oiled and yellow skinned,
                big golden boy and butch king.
                    They call me strap-beast
                    and female masculinity.
                        Come on heritage
                meet this pretty chap in the arena.
                        Are you all bark?
                    I wrestle from the heart.
                They call me stone cold stunner,
                womaniser and pussy jaw-dropper.
                    They call me gentleman
                and jackknife powerbomber.
                        Come on big daddy
                    don't go bailing now on
                    your favourite granddaughter.

ACHILLES:

You, goddess, you alone,
you possess the promised pearl,
the scripts, the seabed ballrooms.
You invented dancing. Before I
knew the word, I only called myself
predator, monster, woman-pretender.
Then you rained cats and dogs!
Tell my mother I am a (REDACTED)

HECATONCHEIRE:

A long goddamn delivery.
The dilations, irregular contractions,
cousin contradictions of incestual relations.
Forgive us. Free us. We should've inherited
the cosmos but like most races were deemed
aliens. Our own mother pretends she was helpless.
Our own mother gave Eden to Cronus.
Our own brother repeated the cycle.
We knew we were not animal as we were herded
like cattle back into vaginal canal. God pretends
not to hear the sound of three hundred fingers
opening up mother earth's stitches.


HERA:

Sons of bitches.


ZEUS:

Who speaks!

MEDEA:

Let me tell you this one thing
and let you never forget it:
if a man does not care when
you bleed out on the ground
before him then there is nothing
you can say or do to make him.

PHILOMELA:

*bird sounds*

The critic is running for his life. Tragedy is quick in pursuit, their massive hands tearing up the incline of the arena. Colonnades come loose under their fingers, and people too, their small bodies ascending to heaven by way of sheer physical labour. The critic sweats and clutches at his chest, which has been bleeding the whole time. His forehead is crying. They brought an army, he realises, sick to the stomach. Or a family. Either way, there are so many of their kind and so few of him. He gets back to his feet, half-stumbling half-running, hand clutched to the hole opening inside him. It has been opening the whole time.

The Tragedies are on his heels, their feet thundering. They are upon him. They move past him. He slows, mouth gaping. They are leaving him behind. How is that possible? He cannot believe he is still alive.

Why?

The hole stretches. Wretched, he stumbles and stares down at it. His skin gives to redness, and in the middle of it, running its nail around the edges, is a finger.

His eyes widen.

ODYSSEUS:

I thought I saw her, Ithaca.
In a dream I saw her. Then
another wave pulled me under.

ITHACA:

Too many years were taken. I held them well, almost too
much so. When it came time to let them go, something
else left. Something was unsaid. Tell me why, even now, I
hear a voice at my window, squeezing in between panes.
Tell me why I still go to listen to the words of a man I can
barely be sure was real. Even if he comes back now, will
he see me? Will he bend at the knee and sink his fingers
into the sand of the beach? Will his fingers find that
brown-depth underneath, and will he breathe in the cool
salty sea? Men come and come and never really see us.
How many generations will it take to heal from this? For
you it was ten, maybe twenty years. Suns will die before
I am avenged. Before I can think about it without pains,
and between them something squeezing. Something was
unsaid. Sons have died for it. The word (oh my heart)
was mine. My ancestors knew it. A man took it. He can
return. His ship can come. But he cannot say it.

EUPHORBOS:

say it
say it
say it
say it
say it
say it
say it
say it
say it
say it
say it
say it
say it
say it
say it
say it
say it
say it
say it
stubborn
spear-headed
darlin
g

HECTOR:

At great personal cost,
I came to deliver this message.
Mothers sleep and daughters pray
but they cannot say it. Husbands
marry and mistresses feel it and
still they cannot say it. Stronger
men than you have died.
Kinder truths have lied.
And I am not kind. Only honest.

CORYPHAEUS:

At great personal cost,
I came to deliver this message.
As I remember it, my mother
rowed us into the ocean.
She pushed me out.
As I remember it,
the beach was brown-deep
and the sea air was cool
and salty. As I remember it
the sky closed over my body,
a rain-water swaddling.
Then I heard the word.
I heard it in your language.

APHRODITE:

What new lonely world
is this?

SAPPHO:

At an asking
of little to nothing,
I wrote this for you.
Early morning, land dawning,
almost like home
if home could perch on your shoulder
like a familiar. If home could rise out of the sea.
Ithaca, lost to history. Odyssey, lost to English.
I can understand, men having moved my own hand
until ink      fragmented      itself    mosaic
of    bad    translations    and    ego
I can understand. Remember, Polyphemus, that even you
are blessed to die in your native country. Some of us
smear ash across the atlas, our shadows wrung out.
Our love wiped out. Will you cross
blank latitudes for sheer longitude?
Will you pinpoint your heart?
When angels emerge from their pearl-births
(as they will) (as they must) will you be there
in a little boat, docking close?